# ASPECTS OF EARLY READING GROWTH

SCHOOLS COUNCIL RESEARCH
AND DEVELOPMENT PROJECT
IN COMPENSATORY EDUCATION

# ASPECTS OF EARLY READING GROWTH

*A Longitudinal Study*

PAT DAVIES AND PHILLIP WILLIAMS

BASIL BLACKWELL · OXFORD

ISBN 0 631 15650 x

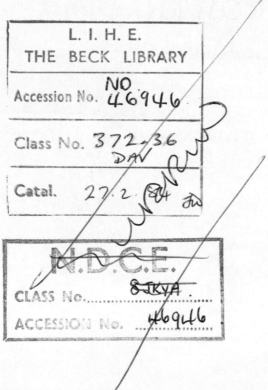
Printed in Great Britain by
Western Printing Services Ltd, Bristol

# Contents

# Acknowledgements

As with the other material produced by the Schools Council Project in Compensatory Education, we wish to acknowledge the kindness and co-operation of the two Education Authorities who participated in the project, the staffs of the schools in which we worked and the children who provided the data. We are also grateful to Lynne Bebb, Roy Evans and Neil Ferguson for their help in the data collection. Michael Rutter made his 'Child Behaviour Scale' available to us, and we do appreciate his willingness to do this. Finally we want to record our thanks to John Merritt for reading and commenting on part of the study and to Joan Whitehead for helping with some of the calculations.

# List of Figures

# List of Tables

CHAPTER 1

# Principles

One of the main aims of the Schools Council Research and
Development Project in Compensatory Education was the construction of a screening device for identifying school entrants
who need special assistance. The development of this device,
the *Swansea Evaluation Profiles* (Evans *et al.*), involved working with a large population of young children, nearly 700 in
all, with whom contact was maintained across the three year
period of their infant schooling. This gave the project team an
opportunity to carry out a longitudinal study of children's development during this period. This longitudinal study was not
one of the project's main aims. But since so little is known about
the educational development of children of this age range, it
seemed wrong to let slip the opportunity of making such a
study. This study reports the results of the growth of two
aspects of early reading skills, considering first overall word-
recognition skill and second the more specific sub-skill of
phonic knowledge.

Since this longitudinal study was an appendix to the main
project, it was of necessity small in scale. A study involving the
whole sample of 700 children could not be mounted, nor was it
possible to attempt to study in detail a large number of aspects
of children's development. So, for logistical reasons, it was
decided to concentrate on a narrowly-focused inquiry, which
studied the development of a small number of specific aspects
of children's educational skills in a small sub-sample of the 700

children. In this way we hoped to be able to provide complementary information to that available from other much larger longitudinal studies, e.g. those of Douglas (1964) and Kellmer Pringle and Davie (1966). These studies have given us much information about children's development, including the growth of children's skills on broad measures of attainment such as standardized tests of reading and number. Our study was aimed at much narrower aspects of attainment.

Not only does this study differ from other longitudinal studies in the specificity of the skills examined, it also differs from them by virtue of the frequency of assessment. The years from five to seven are years of rapid intellectual growth (e.g. Bloom 1964). It seemed important, therefore, to try to increase the frequency with which other investigators have measured children's development across this period, so that the annual or biannual assessments which have characterized many other longitudinal studies could be improved. In this way, more interesting information might be provided. For this reason the sub-sample of children was assessed once each term during the infant school period.

This study differs in yet another way from most studies of children's development, that is in the nature of the measuring instruments used. Most studies have used norm-referenced measuring instruments. For example the Kellmer Pringle and Davie study referred to above used the Southgate scale (Southgate 1959) as a measure of children's reading development. This type of approach is entirely proper, but in the context of this study, focusing on the development of specific skills, there seemed greater advantage in using measures which were 'criterion referenced'. This means measuring the extent to which the children acquired definable skills, rather than comparing their performance with the standardization sample on which an objective test is based. This is an important point which can best be illustrated in relation to another sphere of teaching—physical education. It may be important for a swimming teacher to know something about a child's comparative standard in swimming—for example that his swimming standard is bettered by only 10 per cent of his age group. This is the approach of the norm-referenced test. It is also important for the swimming teacher to know which skills the child has mastered—for example that he has reached the standard of an ASA bronze award. This is the approach of the criterion-referenced test. The translation of the criterion-referenced test from the domain of physical skills, such as swimming, to that of cognitive skills such as reading, is not always straightforward. But is seemed well worth attempting in the context of this study for the following reason.

If the growth of word recognition skills is charted, using a standardized test of word recognition as the measuring instrument, then one can expect, if the groups assessed are representative, a straight-line representation of growth, as shown in Fig. 1.1.

Fig. 1.1 *Development of reading skill as measured by a norm-referenced test*

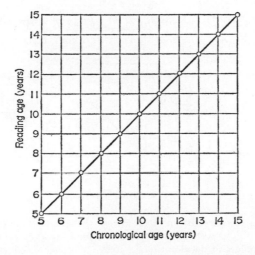

This follows since the average performance of a group of, say, six-year-old children defines a reading age of six years. Similarly, the average performance of eight-year-olds defines a reading age of eight years, and so on. Consequently, one effect of the standardized test approach is deliberately to mask any variations which may be expected to occur at different stages of development. An example from another context may make this clearer.

Tanner (1961) has shown in a simple way the existence of a spurt in physical growth at adolescence. He did this by measuring the height of different age-groups in centimetres, and showing the way in which a rapid increase in height occurs in adolescence. But if he had been using, not a criterion-referenced measure, like a ruler, but a norm-referenced measure which gave the average performances of age-groups, then the existence of the adolescent growth spurt could not have been detected.* The average height of fourteen-year-olds would fall on the straight line of development which norm-referenced instruments entail, as in Fig. 1.2. But the average height for fourteen-year-olds as measured by the centimetre ruler indi-

Fig. 1.2   *Development of height as measured by a (hypothetical) norm-referenced test*

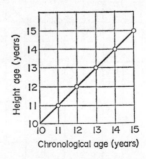

Chronological age (years)

* There may of course be an effect in that the standard deviation of the distribution might well be increased at points of acceleration and decreased at points of deceleration.

cates the existence of a growth spurt at this age, as shown in Fig. 1.3.

Fig. 1.3    *Development of height as measured by a criterion-referenced test (ruler)*

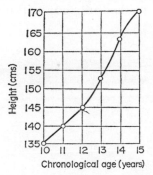

So by using instruments which are criterion-referenced, it is possible to view the development of educational skills in a different light, avoiding the strait-jacketing (important though this is for some purposes) of the norm-referenced measurement device.

These three points, narrow focus, frequent measurement and criterion-referenced instruments, characterized our inquiry in order to provide a somewhat different picture of reading skill development from that which is normally found.

One final point needs stressing. All these three variations could have been applied in a cross-sectional study* It must be remembered that in this study we have applied them in the context of a longitudinal approach. This has the well-known advantages outlined in standard child development textbooks (e.g. Tanner 1961). But the advantage which appealed most to

* A cross-sectional study implies simultaneous measurement of several different groups of the population being studied. For example, in order to determine how children grow physically, the height of age-groups between o and 18 years of age might be measured. It is important to note that a picture of development across childhood can be obtained very rapidly since each age-group consists of different children.

us was the opportunity which longitudinal studies afforded of revealing, more clearly than cross-sectional studies, those periods of rapid change in the rates at which individual children acquire the specific reading skills of this study. This is explained in more detail in Appendix A.

The sample and method of study will now be discussed in the next chapter.

# CHAPTER 2

# Sample and Method

*Construction of the Longitudinal Sub-sample*

The development of the Swansea Evaluation Profiles involved working with a sample of nearly 700 children in two areas, one being a large conurbation and the other a 'county' area. Full details of this sample are given in the Technical Manual for the profiles. From this main sample (see Table 2.1) a sub-sample was chosen to represent a cross-section of school type, sex, age, social class and ability. It was this sub-sample which constituted the group with which this study is concerned. The composition of the sub-sample is described in Tables 2.2 and 2.3 below. Although the original sub-sample consisted of 64 children, one child from area 1 left school without trace during the initial assessments so the final results refer to a sub-sample of 63 children. Originally the sub-sample was based in eight schools, but five children in area 1 moved during the study to other schools in the area.

No child in area 2 moved school during the same period. This reflects the pattern of mobility found in the main study in which 18 per cent of children from area 1 moved, compared with only 4 per cent of children in area 2. One of the main characteristics of area 1 was the amount of mobility of children from schools in deprived areas. This meant that children often left school without leaving any information about their future

B

address.* Some schools from which the longitudinal sub-sample was drawn lost more than half their initial intake during the three infant school years which meant additional problems for the head and class teachers. Some of the gaps in the information collected for the longitudinal sub-sample are due to delays in locating children who moved school without any notification of the area to which they were moving.

Table 2.1   *Location and description of schools in the main sample*

| School Type | Area 1 | Area 2 | Total |
|---|---|---|---|
| Advantaged | 1 | 1 | 2 |
| Settled Working Class | 1 | 1 | 2 |
| Disadvantaged | 4 | 4 | 8 |
| Total | 6 | 6 | 12 |

Although the children were chosen as far as possible to represent a cross-section of social class in advantaged and disadvantaged schools, schools tend to draw their pupils from catchment areas which are usually fairly socially homogeneous. This meant that it was not possible to construct a fully balanced sample (see Table 2.3).

*The Method*

The age of the children involved in the longitudinal study posed certain problems—not only was it difficult to find appropriate measures of development for this age range, but as testing time was limited, tests which required a long time to administer

* Fuller details about the mobility of children in the main sample will be given in the Technical Manual to the *Swansea Evaluation Profiles* (Evans, R.).

were out of the question. It was decided to focus on reading, first because of the obvious importance and emphasis placed on its acquisition in the schools, and secondly because it is an area in which one would reasonably expect there to be a noticeable, measurable development throughout the crucial Infant School years. It was also thought valuable to use the opportunity to trace the development of reading skills in a group of children from relatively deprived backgrounds. For these purposes a graded word reading test (administered individually) and the *Swansea Test of Phonic Skills* (administered individually or in small groups) were chosen to represent two aspects of the reading process.

Table 2.2    *Composition of the longitudinal sub-sample*

| | | Type of School and Area | | | |
|---|---|---|---|---|---|
| | | Advan-taged Area 1 | Advan-taged Area 2 | Dis-advan-taged Area 1 (4 schools) | Dis-advan-taged Area 2 (3 schools) |
| Term of entry | | | | | |
| Autumn term No. of children | 16 | 4 (2 boys + 2 girls) | 4 (2 boys + 2 girls) | 4 (2 boys + 2 girls) | 4 (2 boys + 2 girls) |
| Spring term No. of children | 16 | 4 (2 boys + 2 girls) | 4 (2 boys + 2 girls) | 4 (2 boys + 2 girls) | 4 (2 boys + 2 girls) |
| Summer term No. of children | 32 | 8 (4 boys + 4 girls) | 8 (4 boys + 4 girls) | 8 (4 boys + 4 girls) | 8 (4 boys + 4 girls) |
| Total | 64 | 16 | 16 | 16 | 16 |

Beginning in the Spring term of 1969, the children were examined each term at average intervals of 3–4 months. Children from the Autumn term intake were tested 7 times each and children entering school in the Spring and Summer terms were tested 5 times each. It had been hoped to test all children 7 times but pressure of work with the main sample made this administratively impossible.

Table 2.3    *Social class characteristics of the longitudinal sub-sample* (Occupational Category of Father)

| Occupational category | Advantaged schools | Dis-advantaged schools | Total |
|---|---|---|---|
| 1. Professional | 4 | 0 | 4 |
| 2. Managerial | 5 | 2 | 7 |
| 3. Skilled manual | 15 | 12 | 27 |
| 4. Semi-skilled manual | 4 | 6 | 10 |
| 5. Unskilled | 1 | 6 | 7 |
| 6. Father missing | 2 | 5 | 7 |
| 7. Missing information | 0 | 1 | 1 |
| Total | 31 | 32 | 63 |

The average age of the sub-sample at the time of the first assessments was 5.6* with a range of 5.3 to 5.11. The average on the fifth occasion was 6.9 with a range of 6.5 to 7.3. The average on the seventh occasion was 7.4.

Assessments for the longitudinal study did not start until each child had been assessed, during his first term at school, on the series of developmental tests carried out for the main study. By the time the first assessments of the longitudinal study were made the children had been in school for about six months. As the testers had already seen each child several times during

* Throughout this report ages will be referred to in the following way, e.g. 5.3 means an age of 5 years 3 months.

the course of the assessments for the main study, there were no real problems of rapport because the testers were already familiar figures to the children. Most children were eager to participate and many enjoyed the extra attention.

Four testers were involved in these assessments although most of the assessments were made by two testers. This meant that normally the children were seen by the same tester on each occasion. Although this was not always possible this was not thought to be a problem because of the high reliability of the tests. Throughout the assessment children were encouraged to do their best, but were never told when they had made a mistake and their mistakes were not corrected.

During the last term of infant schooling, each child in the main sample was given the Raven *Coloured Matrices* test. This is often described as a test of non-verbal intelligence which gives a useful indication of the children's ability in an area markedly different from school attainment.

Information about the home background of each child in the main sample was collected by the head teacher, or, if parents were unable or unwilling to attend the school for an interview, with the help of health visitors. Each parent received a letter explaining the purpose of the research and asking for their co-operation and permission to test the child. Comparatively few parents refused to take part. This information provided some of the background to the case studies.

Children in the longitudinal sub-sample were not specifically chosen to constitute a 'disadvantaged' group and there is in fact a fairly normal distribution of social class within the sub-sample. However, it must be remembered that half of the sub-sample came from schools in disadvantaged areas and although obviously not all these children were educationally disadvantaged (similarly some children from advantaged area schools were in some respects educationally disadvantaged) these children tended to have far more disadvantaging factors in their backgrounds than their counterparts in advantaged area schools. When we talk of disadvantaging factors we refer not only to financial difficulties and poor amenities in the home, but to very large families, families where the father was missing, lack of parental interest in the child's education and the poor educational and cultural background of the parents.

# CHAPTER 3

# Growth of Word Recognition Skills

## Introduction

There is an enormous amount of literature on the processes which children use to acquire word recognition skills. There is also an enormous amount of literature on the relative effects of different methods of teaching the early stages of reading, in which word recognition is often one of the criteria on which the success of different methods is compared. (See, for example, Otto *et al.*, 1972.) But although word recognition is one of the fundamental skills in the early stages of reading, there have been very few attempts to plot the way in which word recognition develops in children learning to read the English language. In a previous inquiry by one of the authors, Williams (1961) found that there is a period of relatively gentle acquisition of word recognition skills between the ages of five and seven years, followed by a period of somewhat more rapid acquisition of word recognition skills between the ages of seven and nine years, after which the rate of acquisition gradually diminishes. The picture on which this description is based appears in Fig. 3.1. (The scale used to measure word recognition is discussed below.)

But this earlier study used a cross-sectional approach and so did not do justice to the much greater individual variations in reading growth which a longitudinal study might reveal, for the reasons outlined in Appendix A. So in this present chapter we intend to report those findings on the development of word recognition skills in young children which are revealed by the use of the specific procedures of this study.

Fig. 3.1    *Growth of word recognition skills*

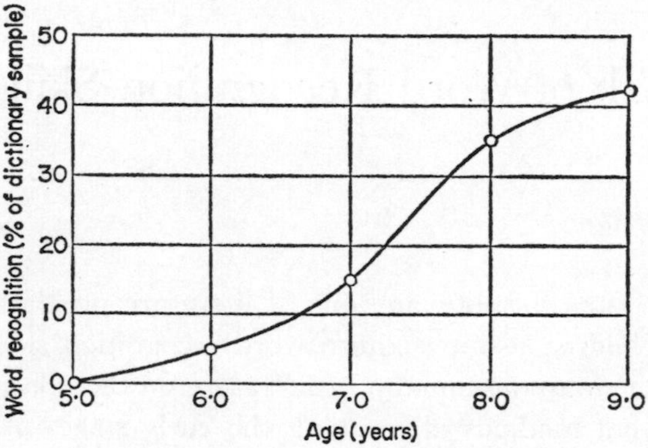

*The Test*

It was decided to follow a well-used method of measuring word recognition skill by requiring children to pronounce single words. An approach which originated in earlier work on the acquisition of spoken vocabulary and which differs from the conventional age-scale approach of tests of word recognition, was used to construct the scale. The development of word recognition proficiency in the sub-sample was assessed by a scale which is a sample of one hundred words selected from a dictionary, in this case the Concise Oxford Dictionary. The advantage of this approach is that a score on such a scale can be instantly converted to a proportion of the dictionary vocabulary which the reader can be expected to recognize (or more accurately, recognize and pronounce correctly). Thus a child with a score of 20 words correct can be expected to recognize 20 per cent of the words of the dictionary. This—proportion of the dictionary performance—is the criterion against which word recognition proficiency is assessed, rather than the average performances of age groups.

The test, therefore, consists of a set of one hundred words, randomly selected from the Concise Oxford Dictionary, and arranged in order of difficulty (previously assessed) on a prepared card. The way in which the sampling was carried out, the reliability of the scale,* and the composition of the scale itself, are given in the details relating to Scale A in Williams (1961), where the validity of the scale as a reasonable and representative sample of the dictionary vocabulary is also discussed.

## Methods of administration

The method of administration of this scale is similar to that of any of the standard word recognition tests, e.g. the Schonell or the Burt/Vernon scales. After establishing rapport, the child is asked to read as many of the words as he can. The assessment is ended when he is unable accurately to pronounce ten words in sequence.**

The scales were not made available to anyone other than project testers in order to minimize the possibility of any coaching, conscious or unconscious, affecting the scores which the children obtained in the later assessments.

## Results

### INDIVIDUAL GROWTH CURVE

In order to explore the pattern in which word recognition skills are required we plotted the scores of each child on the test described above.

* The reliability, as might be expected, was high. For a sample of 50 schedules a split half reliability calculation gave r = + 0.98.
** Copies of the scale can be obtained from the second author at the Open University.

Fig. 3.2 is an example of a reasonably typical growth curve. Note that it supports the view that development can be described as falling into three main phases. First, a slow rate of acquisition of word recognition skills: second, a period of rapid growth or growth spurt: third, a slackening of rate. Note also how much more rapid is the growth spurt revealed by this longitudinal method of study. Compare the growth of Figs. 3.1 and 3.2. This S-shaped or ogive-type curve of growth was present in complete or incomplete form in nearly all the children. There were, of course, variations of different kinds, two examples of which are shown in Figs. 3.3 and 3.4 respectively.

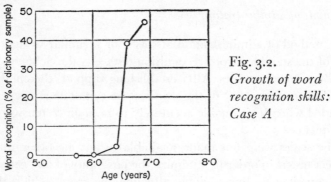

Fig. 3.2.
*Growth of word recognition skills: Case A*

*Fig. 3.3* is an example of a child who was unable to make any start with word recognition skills across the whole period of assessments.

*Fig. 3.4* is an example of a child who, on entry to infant school, had already acquired a high word recognition vocabulary. (Many teachers will recognize the cases illustrated in Figs. 3.3 and 3.4 as examples of children they have themselves met. They will also realize that the high word recognition skill shown by the child in Fig. 3.4 does not necessarily imply great success in reading in the full sense of the word.)

Some children had made a start with the acquisition of word recognition skills, but had not completed their path along the reading development ogive. Fig. 3.5 is an example of a child in this category.

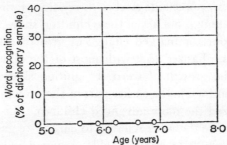

Fig. 3.3.
*Growth of word recognition skills: Case B*

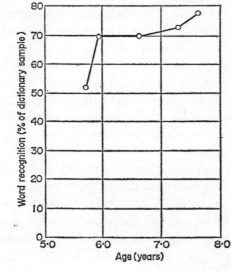

Fig. 3.4.
*Growth of word recognition skills: Case C*

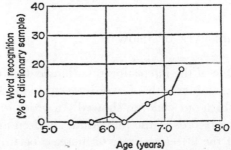

Fig. 3.5.
*Growth of word recognition skills: Case D*

But by and large, our inspection of the word recognition development of those children in this sub-sample who had made an appreciable start with reading, indicated that the majority (though not all) of these children showed a clearly recognizable spurt or marked change of growth rate. It must however be emphasized that with most of the children in this sub-sample the growth of word recognition skills was proceeding slowly and fell in the earlier part of the growth ogive which characterized the more advanced children. This is only to be expected, since the work referred to earlier suggested that the most rapid growth in reading skills occurred with children between the reading ages of 7 and 8 years and it is only the more advanced of this particular sub-sample of children who can be expected to have entered that particular developmental stage.

It is therefore clear that for the majority of children studied, word recognition skills grew at a slow and steady rate across the period, as in Fig. 3.5. But a proportion of the children, the more advanced group, had made their way up the word recognition growth curve until they entered the more interesting stage of the reading spurt.

In all, fifteen children had, by the end of our study, reached a word recognition skill of 30 per cent of dictionary sample or more. These fifteen provide interesting information which helps to answer a number of specific questions about the size and duration of the word recognition spurt. It is to these questions that we now turn.

THE RATE OF GROWTH

One of the interesting questions is that of the steepness of the rate of growth of word recognition skills during the spurt which our children showed. In order to do this, we examined the records of the individual children and calculated for each of the fifteen the rate of increase occurring between each pair

of points at which word recognition was assessed. It is appreci-
ated that this does not necessarily give the best measure of the
maximum velocity of growth, but a more sophisticated
approach would have involved an exercise in curve fitting
which seemed unnecessarily refined for the simple data with
which we were dealing. An example of the way in which the
calculations were carried out is given for Case E.

Table 3.1    *Rate of growth calculations for Case E*

| a | b | c | d | e | f |
|---|---|---|---|---|---|
| Occasion of test | Word recognition ( % of dictionary sample) | Interval between occasions | Time in months | Increase in word recognition skills ( %) | Annual rate of increase e/d × 12 |
| 1 | 0 | | | | |
| 2 | 0 | 1 and 2 | 4 | 0 | 0 |
| 3 | 1 | 2 and 3 | 5 | 1 | 2 |
| 4 | 2 | 3 and 4 | 3 | 1 | 4 |
| 5 | 19 | 4 and 5 | 4 | 17 | 51 |
| 6 | 36 | 5 and 6 | 5 | 17 | 41 |
| 7 | 40 | 6 and 7 | 3 | 4 | 16 |

In this way we obtained for each of the fifteen children a
measure of the rate of acquisition of word recognition skills
at different points during the three-year period across which
they were studied. We then recorded the maximum rate of
acquisition which each one of these children showed. These
maximum velocities are shown below in Table 3.2.

It is interesting to note that the modal maximum velocity,
that is the most frequently attained maximum velocity, falls in
the '60 per cent–70 per cent of dictionary per year' cell. This

indicates that most children show a growth spurt which, at its maximum, proceeds at a very high rate. If this rate were to be prolonged, it would result in between two-thirds and three-quarters of the total dictionary vocabulary being added to their word recognition repertoire within a year. Naturally this rate is not sustained, but it does indicate the enormous speed at which word recognition skills are developed for short periods of time.

Table 3.2    *Maximum velocities of word recognition acquisition*

| Maximum rate of growth (% of dictionary per year) | 0–19 | 20–39 | 40–59 | 60–79 | 80–99 | 100–119 | 120+ |
|---|---|---|---|---|---|---|---|
| No. of children | 0 | 0 | 4 | 8 | 1 | 0 | 2 |

Even more interesting is the last cell, which indicates that for two children there was a period during which the rate of acquisition of word recognition skills was proceeding at a rate of over 120 per cent of dictionary vocabulary per year. This rate could not have been sustained for any length of time! But it does emphasize very clearly the rapid speed at which word recognition skills, once a basis is acquired, can be built on and developed by children going through these earlier stages of reading growth. The belief that word recognition development is a steady process, as seems to be implied by norm-based word recognition tests, is clearly seen to be inaccurate.

THE POINT AT WHICH PEAK RATE OCCURS

Another interesting question is to ask when this maximum rate of acquisition occurs. In order to do this we looked at the figures for maximum growth and related them to the size of the word recognition vocabulary at the time. The results of this are given in Table 3.3.

Table 3.3    *Size of word recognition vocabulary when rate of acquisition is at maximum*

| Size of word recognition vocabulary at maximum growth rate (% of dictionary) | 0–9 | 10–19 | 20–29 | 30–39 | 40–49 |
|---|---|---|---|---|---|
| No. of children | 0 | 4 | 8 | 1 | 2 |

This indicates that for most children the peak of word recognition growth occurs when the word recognition vocabulary is between 20 per cent and 29 per cent, or roughly a quarter of dictionary vocabulary.

When the child has acquired about 25 per cent of dictionary vocabulary, his rate of growth is proceeding very rapidly and shortly after that, within the space of a few months, the growth of his word recognition skills starts to tail off.

*Discussion*

There are several points which can be made in relation to the findings. First, let us consider those theoretical points which relate to the methods of study used. The introduction to this study suggested that if educational development were measured by methods which differ from those of the norm-based tests, then the stages of educational growth might be seen in a new light. This is most clearly shown if one compares the model of word recognition growth illustrated in Fig. 1.1 with the alternative model of Fig. 3.1. Measurement of the first sort misses the difference in the growths which occur at different periods. An improvement of one year of reading age across the period 5 to 6 years is entirely different from the improvement of one year of reading age across the reading age-span 7 to 8 years. A criterion-referenced method of assessment demonstrates clearly the relative variation between skill growth at different ages. Additionally however, when this method of assessment is used in conjunction with frequent observations and a longitudinal approach, it can reveal the immense changes in development whch individual children show. These are the interesting growth-spurts summarized in Table 3.2 and which cross-sectional approaches mask.

One note of warning needs to be sounded. The composition of the sub-sample of children has been described in Chapter 2. Although the social class structure of the sub-sample is not too distorted, nevertheless it must be remembered that half the children are pupils in disadvantaged schools. So the individual children who showed the word recognition spurt are necessarily those who are 'advanced readers' in the context of our sub-sample. It may be, though we think it unlikely, that marked spurts are characteristics of advanced readers in particular backgrounds only. This remains to be determined by other inquiries.

A little more doubt can be expressed about the point at which the maximum rate of word recognition growth occurs (Table 3.3). Since we included for this purpose all children with word recognition skills as low as 30 per cent on the last assessment, there is likely to be some underestimate of the point of maximum rate. Once again, the extent of this remains to be determined by other inquiries.

Theoretical points such as these lead on to the more practical questions which follow. What changes occur to the other reading skills which a child acquires when the rate of growth of word recognition fluctuates? What are the sub-skills which underlie the spurt, and why does the spurt diminish at approximately (we suspect) 60 per cent of dictionary sample?

We have no real answer to these points. We could, for example, erect a model which suggests that the early stages of the word recognition growth curve are associated with the development of simple visual methods of word recognition. As the child enters a period of increasing growth, he is acquiring, on this model, those phonic patterns which enable him to deal with the common regularities of the language. His travel up the growth spurt of word recognition may well be linked to the establishment of syllabication and other higher order skills. The tailing-off period may take place when an increase in word recognition skills comes to depend more and more on the mastery of irregularities.

This is a simple 'language-structure' model of word recognition growth. It pays no attention to other influences affecting word recognition growth. For example, the sorts of language experience which children enjoy may afford a different model for explaining word recognition growth: so may the kinds of teaching experience provided.

But the design of our study limited us to exploring questions related to the first model only. So we turn now to the second major aspect of the growth of reading skills which was examined, the development of phonic skills in the sub-sample of children in our study. This follows in the next chapter.

C

## CHAPTER 4

# The Growth of Phonic Skills

*Introduction*

Although there are many skills involved in the reading process, a child's success in reading will depend to a large extent on his having a successful method of tackling new words. The child who does not have some understanding of phonics, of the correct pronunciation of letters and common letter combinations (graphemes) will only be able to guess at the pronunciation of new words. He may then be in the position of being able to 'read' the word 'aeroplane' because he recognizes it, but completely unable to tackle a simple word which he has never met before, such as 'shop'.

*The Test*

It is more difficult to assess a child's phonic ability than his ability to recognize words. Even if a child successfully reads a word containing the grapheme we wish to test, we do not know whether he really can pronounce the grapheme correctly or whether he is merely recognizing a word which is already within his reading vocabulary. For example, he may read the word 'ship' which starts with the grapheme 'sh' without necessarily knowing the sound value (or phoneme) associated with

'sh'. The way in which this difficulty was overcome was by
using a test which consists of a set of nonsense words containing the graphemes to be tested. This means that the child's
phonic skills can be tested without interference; his score cannot reflect his ability to recognize word patterns as the nonsense
words are new to him.

But there is another difficulty in this approach. If a child
is unable to read, for example, 'sheb', we do not know
whether he failed because he was genuinely unfamiliar with
the grapheme 'sh'. It might be that he is ignorant of the 'eb'
combination, or perhaps misled by the 'she' configuration. To
a large extent this problem can be overcome if the child is
presented with a set of nonsense words all of which end in 'eb'
but which differ in the initial grapheme, e.g., cheb, steb, gleb,
creb. If the child is now asked by the examiner to identify
'sheb' we can be much more sure (though not certain) whether
or not he is aware of the correct pronunciation of the grapheme 'sh'. This is the principle, that of choice from a set of nonsense words, differing only in the grapheme being tested, which
underlies the test to assess the development of phonic skills.
While the test used does not cover all possible graphemes it
does cover most commonly met graphemes.*

The test consists of 65 items divided into 5 sections; short
vowels, long vowels, initial letter blends, final letter blends and
a miscellaneous section which includes vowel combinations,
consonant digraphs initial position, and consonant digraphs
final position. Each item consists of 5 nonsense words (see Fig.
4.1) one of which is the word (pok) containing the grapheme
('p') to be tested and 4 decoys. The position of the word to be
identified is altered at random for each item.

---

* For details of the construction, reliability, diagnostic use and full
details of the administration of the test see the teacher's manual to the
*Swansea Test of Phonic Skills* (Williams, P., 1970).

Fig. 4.1    *Practice Item 1*

---

wok
lok
mok
rok
pok

## *Method of Administration*

The test can be administered in small groups or individually. Where possible group administration was used, although when individual children moved to new schools or when children had been absent from school the test was administered individually. Each child is given a test booklet and pencil and told that he is going to play a game. There are two practice items during which the tester ensures that every child understands what he has to do. Then, for each item, the tester says the test word once while the child locates the word and identifies it by drawing a ring round it.

## *Growth of Phonic Skills*

The standardization data of the test indicate the rate at which children acquire the phonic skills it tests. This is shown in Fig. 4.2. The data also permit a preliminary analysis of the relative difficulty which children experience with different phonic elements. This difficulty order appears in the manual to the test, and is presented in diagram form in Appendix C.

Note that the data given in Fig. 4.2 refer only to the period across which children are acquiring skills rapidly—the growth spurt period. Before and after this period of gentle but steady increase in phonic proficiency the growth rate must, of course, flatten. As in the previous chapter, we now examine the variations from this growth pattern which a longitudinal study might reveal.

Fig. 4.2.
*Acquisition of
phonic skills*

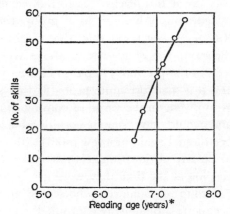

*Based on norms from the Southgate
reading test.

*Results*

## OVERALL PATTERN OF RESULTS

The results of the sub-sample as a whole fall into three broad groups.

Group (i) Children who scored 0 on all occasions: these were children who, unable to cope with what was required, either failed to complete the test or showed a patterned response, putting a ring around every second word for example. As might have been expected these 14 children are characterized by having considerably lower scores on the Raven matrices test and by coming from homes of lower social class (as measured by the Registrar General's classification of social class) than children from groups (ii) and (iii).

Group (ii) Children who scored at least 1 but less than 29 on each of the test occasions: the constructors of the phonics test consider that if a child scores below 29 he is generally weak

in all phonic skills. This group of 15 children consists therefore
of children who showed little progress during the period of
assessment. It is difficult to look at these scores in a meaningful
way, as at this level of performance scores are often affected
by guessing. Although as a group their mean score on the
Raven test was lower than that of group (iii), each member of
the group was of average or above average ability. As we have
seen in the previous chapter, children progress at uneven rates
and it is therefore quite probable that several members of this
group were on the verge of coming to terms with phonic skills
and would have shown considerable development had they
been tested again in a few months' time. There did not appear
to be any obvious intellectual reason why they were not suc-
ceeding at the time they were last tested.

Group (iii) Children who scored 29 or more on at least one
occasion: although as a group these 34 children had higher
mean scores on the Raven test and were from homes of
higher social and economic status than children from groups
(i) and (ii) not all of the group appeared to be educationally
advantaged. For example, four children came from homes
where the father was semi-skilled, four from homes where
the father unskilled and two children were from fatherless
families. One child was from one of the most disadvantaged
families in the whole study. (See Case Study 1.)

The mean differences between the three groups are shown
in Table 4.1.

Table 4.1    *Mean scores on Raven matrices and the mean
socio-economic status of three groups of children*

|  | Mean score on Ravens | Mean socio-economic status |
|---|---|---|
| Group 1 | 15.3 | 5.3 |
| Group 2 | 19.4 | 4.5 |
| Group 3 | 25.1 | 3.9 |

The overlaps between the groups are as interesting as the differences between them. Once we move away from examining group trends to looking at individuals the reasons why some succeed and others fail are extremely complex. This can be seen in more detail when looking at the case studies in Chapter 5.

INDIVIDUAL RATES OF GROWTH

As our main purpose in this chapter is to trace the development of phonic skills, it is more useful to focus attention on the 34 children in group (iii) where we can more clearly see the overall pattern of development. In this group, development can be traced from very low levels of performance to a considerable degree of skill.

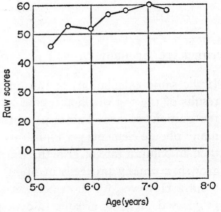

Fig. 4.3.
*Growth of phonic
skills: Case F*

Of the 34 children, 9 scored 29 or more on 5 occasions, 9 on 14 occasions, 10 on 2 occasions and 6 on one occasion. The group demonstrates a range of development, from children who had already acquired considerable phonic skills before the first assessment was made (see Fig. 4.3) to children who did not reach this level of performance until they were almost ready to transfer to the junior school (see Fig. 4.4).

Case F performed well above the mean for the group from

the beginning and was well advanced phonically. She had probably passed her peak rate of growth before the time that she was first assessed. Case J was phonically weak until the last few months when she started making rapid progress.

Fig. 4.4.
*Growth of phonic
skills: Case J*

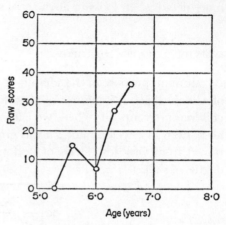

THE RATE OF GROWTH

If the same calculations of rate of growth are made for the results of the test of phonic skills as were made for the word recognition test—see Tables 3.1 and 3.2—we can calculate how many phonic elements per month were acquired by children at their maximum rate of growth. We can see from Fig. 4.2 that growth normally proceeds at about 3.5 phonic elements per month. However, for short periods of time individual children progressed at a far greater rate of growth as we can see in Table 4.2.

Table 4.2    *Maximum velocities of the acquisition of
phonic skills*

| Maximum rate of growth (No. of phonic elements per month) | 0–5 | 6–10 | 11–15 | 12–20 |
|---|---|---|---|---|
| No. of children | 20 | 10 | 2 | 1 |

The majority of children acquired between 1 and 5 phonic elements per month. But a good proportion, between $\frac{1}{3}$ and $\frac{1}{2}$, were acquiring skills at a rate of 6 or more elements per month, or over 72 per year, were it possible to maintain this rate of growth. One child only showed no growth (see Case Study IV). He was a very advanced reader at 5+ and kept a constant score of 60. One child (see Fig. 4.5 and Case Study II) at her

Fig. 4.5.
*Growth of phonic
skills: Case K*

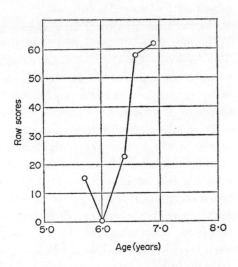

maximum rate of growth acquired 37 phonic elements in 2 months. K was an exceptional case who suddenly, for no apparent reason, dramatically improved in her school work, especially in reading skill. This is particularly interesting since she was frequently absent from school. These absences led to the unusually long period of 5 months between one pair of assessments in Fig. 4.5.

In this particular group of children there was no obvious point at which the maximum rate of growth of phonic skills occurred (see Table 4.3). Indeed it would be somewhat surprising to have found this, although there is a slight tendency for maximum growth to be more connected with the lower

Table 4.3    *Size of scores on test of phonic skills
when rate of acquisition is at maximum*

| Score | 0–10 | 11–20 | 21–30 | 31–40 | 41–50 |
|---|---|---|---|---|---|
| No. of Children | 8 | 8 | 7 | 5 | 5 |

range of scores. Only 5 children showed a spurt in development after they had scored 40 or more.

As we have already stated, Tables 4.2 and 4.3 refer only to maximum rates of growth during the period of assessments. The figures refer only to children who were phonically advanced, compared with other children in the longitudinal subsample, and therefore it is possible that there were even greater spurts of development before these children were first assessed.

It is interesting in this connection to look at the phonic scores of the 15 advanced readers discussed in the previous chapter. If we look at the *occasion* on which all these 15 children first reached a score of 30 per cent or more on the word recognition test (their average score on this occasion was 38.6 per cent) we see that their average score then on the test of phonic skills was 57.6. That is, they were scoring at a very high level indeed on this test before they reached a reasonable level of skill.

The occasion of maximum rate of growth on both tests coincides for only 4 of the 15 children. The remaining 11 children reach their maximum rate of growth in phonic skills before their maximum rate of growth in word recognition skills. No child showed maximum growth of word recognition skills *before* maximum growth of phonic skills. As we suggested in the introduction to this chapter, it seems that a child needs considerable understanding of phonics before he is able to demonstrate reasonable success in word recognition skills.

*Discussion*

Only just over half of the children in the longitudinal sub-sample attained any degree of phonic ability, defined as a score of 29 or more on the test used, during their period of infant schooling. This is partly explained by the nature of the sample, which is somewhat biased towards disadvantaged children. To balance this however, a number of children reached a considerable level of skill, some of them reaching a high level of attainment right at the beginning of their infant schooling.

A picture of development in phonic skills similar to that seen in the development of word recognition emerged. For short periods of time most children showed rates of growth which were considerably faster than that indicated by the cross-sectional data of Fig. 4.2. This was regardless of at what stage in their development they were first assessed, but obviously to obtain a clearer view of the pattern, a larger sample would have to be studied and if possible for an extended period.

There was no clear picture of when this growth spurt occurs except that there was an indication that it occurs at an early rather than at a late stage in the child's acquisition of phonic skills. The reasons for this are not clear and may in part be related to the nature of the test. Obviously the 65 test items are not all of the same difficulty level and therefore success in the later stages may depend on mastery of more irregular forms which are more slowly acquired. Again, to determine whether or not there is a pattern in the timing and length of growth spurts a larger study would have to be undertaken.

On a basis of the examination of the results of the 'advanced readers' it would appear that children did not reach a reasonable level of word recognition until they had acquired a fairly high level of phonic skills. Neither did the growth spurt in word recognition skills occur until the spurt in phonic skills was passed. Again, more detailed studies of individual development may clarify the relationship between the growth of phonic skills and word recognition. This would appear to be an area of study worthy of further investigation when there is so much discussion about the place of phonics in the overall reading process.

# CHAPTER 5

# Case Studies

I. Me and Br were non-identical twins from a poor home. Whereas Me fell further and further behind Br began to improve considerably.

Me and Br were the eighth and ninth children of a family of twelve whose father had deserted them. Before the children entered school (in deprived area 1) the family had lived for some time in a hostel. Their present home conditions were described by the health visitor as 'appalling'. Not surprisingly the mother did not attend the school to answer questions about the home, so little detailed information was available. Their class teachers were impressed by the cheerfulness and patience shown by the twins' mother in spite of her difficulties.

When they were 5.0 the twins were below average weight—'poor little scraps' in the words of the doctor. Br had mild conjunctivitis and her hair was falling out; she was one of the very few children from the main sample whose physical condition was said to be unsatisfactory. Both children were dirty and had been cleansed for this reason.

The children were often absent from school for trivial reasons and Br's class teacher said, 'Br is so often absent that she tends to be far behind other children in the class. This does not appear to worry her. If she cannot do what she is asked, she just "doesn't want to know".' Br lacked concentration, told lies and sometimes stole things; the teacher forecast that she would be in need of extra help in a normal class through a remedial teacher by the time she was 8. Me's class teacher listed many behaviour problems such as extreme restlessness, stealing, bullying, fighting and destroying property. He too lacked concentration and in addition to his rather aggressive behaviour he worried, often appeared miserable, bit his finger nails and was not much liked by the other children. He also had speech difficulties and his teacher predicted that he would be in need of a full-time special class or class for slow learners by the time he was 8.

At 5.0 Br had better results on the developmental tests than her brother and was slightly ahead of him after the first batch of longitudinal tests. By the time the twins were 7.0 Br had improved all round. She was cleaner and healthier and had settled well into school, appearing to enjoy it considerably. Although she will continue to have frequent absences of one or two days her reading age at 7.0 was average. But Me could still not read (although he was a member of a remedial reading class) and was well below average in all aspects of language and number. He had not adjusted to school as well as his sister, he still lacked concentration, was not much liked by other children and tended to be fearful of new things or situations. His speech was difficult to understand because of marked immaturity and poor education and he had very poor powers of oral expression, although he was always very friendly and ready to talk.

The test of non-verbal intelligence placed Br as slightly above average and Me as of very low intelligence. Although this might explain the widening gap between the performances of the twins it does not altogether explain Br's dramatic improvement. At 5.0 she was ranked 442nd out of 627 on the developmental tests given to the main sample; at 7.0 she was 288th.

The intellectual differences between the twins are obvious. In addition, Me had many more emotional problems than his sister which, added to the condition of his home, more than accounts for his very low performance. In spite of the poor physical conditions of her home Br's good adjustment to school enabled her to enjoy school. She was interested in school activities and with the encouragement of her teacher was able to reach good average attainment. Her future, when difficult circumstances and cultural poverty at home are likely to have more influence on her attainment, is uncertain.

II. Di and Jo were of the same non-verbal intelligence and from similar homes, but whereas Di improved Jo deteriorated.

Both girls were second children whose fathers were labourers at a steelworks in area 2. Di attended a school in a disadvantaged area, whereas Jo attended a school in an advantaged area.

Jo was born prematurely with a hole in her heart. Her mother admitted that she had been over-protective because of her anxieties about Jo's medical condition. These anxieties seem to have been communicated to Jo who was described by her teacher as very often worried, miserable and tearful, especially on arrival at school, and fearful of new things and situations. In spite of this she settled into school very well and had many friends. Her class teacher predicted that she would be in need of extra help in a normal classroom by the time she was 8; at 7.0 she was below average in language and number skills and was still considered to be in need of special help. Although Jo's parents had both left school before 16 they wanted her to stay at school until she was 18.

Di's mother suffered from nervous trouble which may have contributed to Di's tendency to worry and be afraid—she was still enuretic when she started school. Although Di's father had the same type of job as Jo's, the head teacher of Di's school thought that the family was only 'just managing'. Di's mother did some paid housework for a few hours each week. The physical amenities of the house were not good, with no fixed bath, no hot water from a tap and no indoor toilet. Yet Di always came to school clean and attractively dressed. Her parents had both completed their education at 14 but said they wanted Di to stay at school until 18. She settled into school very well and her class teacher predicted that she would be a good pupil.

The greatest difference in their attainment was in reading. Jo had still not learned to read by the end of the infant school whereas Di had a reading age above her chronological age. It is not surprising that Jo had deteriorated. She had experienced not only frequent short term absences (sometimes attending the morning session only) but also some prolonged absences from school, when she was in hospital undergoing heart operations.

As in the case of the twins Me and Br, it is easier to explain failure than success. During the infant school years, Di's ability to read took her far above the average performance for the sample as a whole. Her class teacher was very pleased with Di's progress and surprised at her sudden spurt in spite of fairly frequent absences of short duration. The physical conditions of Di's home were not ideal nor was it very cultured. Her mother tended to keep Di at home for trivial reasons and yet she was forging ahead. As in the case of Br the main factors in her success seem to be enjoyment of school, interest in learning—especially reading—and an encouraging teacher. It is only to be hoped that this pattern will be maintained.

III. Pq was an intelligent child who so far had failed to learn to read, although coming from a supportive family.

Pq's father was in a skilled manual occupation having served a full-time apprenticeship. The family was thought to be financially secure and lived in privately owned property with good physical amenities although the area was nominated by the local education authority as deprived. Both parents were very interested in Pq's education. They had a good relationship with his school and hoped that Pq would stay at school until he was 18. They thought that Pq was happy at school and doing well.

Pq started school at 4.8 years after having attended for the previous year the nursery school attached. His reception class teacher said that Pq had settled into school very well, but added, 'Pq is rather a defiant child, although I have found him quite interesting and intelligent'. Pq had sometimes destroyed things in the classroom, fought and bullied other children and told lies. He was very restless, often disobedient. He had few friends, probably because of his rather anti-social behaviour.

His teacher predicted that he would be an exceptionally good pupil and this was confirmed by his high ranking on the developmental tests. The results of the first longitudinal tests showed that, in common with most of the sample, he could not read. But examination of his class work showed that his vocabulary and understanding of number concepts were above average. This pattern of results did not change throughout his infant schooling, so that at 7.0 he could read only a few words, although his vocabulary and language were still well above average. On the Raven test his score was well above average.

One of Pq's parents belonged to the library and both were interested in reading. They frequently read to Pq and said that Pq often 'read' to himself. His definitions of words reveal an imagination not often shown by other children in the sample even though there were children of greater all-round ability. He defined a hero as 'a man who has been fighting against a lot of other men by himself with only a rolling pin. He gets a medal.' An umbrella is 'something that when it is raining you put up over your head to keep you dry. Sometimes little boys try to use them as parachutes.' He said that a 'spade' is one of the suits of 'cards', and 'very useful if you are going to bury someone'.

It is surprising that in spite of his fluency and obvious interest in words and stories he had not learned to read. One would have expected him to have an interest in reading which would have enabled him to succeed. In the last term of the infant

D

school his class teacher said that he tended to lack concentration and to be disobedient. He often appeared miserable or unhappy, frequently sucked his thumb and was nearly always alone as he had no friends and did not attempt to make any. He was not much liked by his teacher who said he was spiteful to other children and rather sly in trying to get others into trouble.

Pq was a regular attender at school and had a good medical record so without further more detailed information it is impossible to give the reasons for his failure to read. There is the possibility that it was connected with emotional difficulties and his failure to make successful relationships with his fellow pupils. Clearly he is a child who needs educational help, perhaps from the remedial teaching service.

IV. Ck was an able child from a financially poor home in a deprived area who had understanding and encouraging parents. His attainment level was high.

When Ck started school in disadvantaged area 1, his father was employed as a machinist although there was some record of him having previously had a clerical occupation. The physical amenities of the home were not good; there was no fixed bath, no hot water from a tap and no indoor w.c.

Ck's parents said that they had tried to teach Ck before he started school; by the time he started school he could read a whole sentence, write his name and was good at counting. He had been longing to go to school. His class teacher said that he settled in very well and showed no problems of behaviour at all. His teacher predicted that he would be an exceptionally good pupil.

At 5.0, Ck ranked 5/627 on developmental tests showing above average development in all areas.

During Ck's first year at school his parents were interviewed by the project social worker. At this time Ck's father was out of work but in spite of this the home was undoubtedly secure and happy with much interest shown in the three children one of whom was physically handicapped. Neither of Ck's parents had been educated beyond the age of 16 but both showed great interest in his education and wanted him to stay at school until 18. They were very definite in the view that they preferred him to have a good education and a poorly paid job than a poor education and a well paid job.

During Ck's second year at school his parents moved to a new housing estate which considerably improved the physical conditions of the home.

When he was 7.8 he had a reading age of 9.9 on the Holborn sentence reading test and a reading age of 12.4 on the Burt graded word reading test. His matrices test score placed him in the intellectually superior section of the population. When he was first tested at 5.8 he read 55 words (which he later increased to 83) and he scored 60 on the test of phonic skills.

Ck is an example of a child of high ability whose parents, although not well educated themselves, were very interested in his education, encouraging and helping him whenever possible. He thoroughly enjoyed school where he was given a great deal of encouragement. These factors were far more important in determining Ck's progress and attainment than the fact that at first the material conditions of the home had not been good and that the father's periods of unemployment had caused the family some financial hardship.

# Appendix A

*The advantages of using longitudinal*
*studies in revealing growth spurts*

The advantage of using longitudinal studies in revealing growth spurts applies because children start growth spurts at different ages. Adolescents, for example, do not all start their physical growth spurt at 13 years of age exactly. One child may be an early maturer, whose growth spurt starts at 10 years of age. Another may be a later maturer, whose growth spurt starts at 16 years of age. This variation has a considerable masking effect on the rates of growth obtained by studies which use a cross-sectional approach. An example may make this clearer.

Consider a study which decides to assess the physical growth of children across the ages 10 to 16. Suppose that one study decides to use the cross-sectional aproach, and sets up a mini-sample of three children at each of four age groups, 10 year olds, 12 year olds, 14 year olds and 16 year olds. Let us further suppose that the three children chosen at each age group consist of an early maturer (E), a later maturer (L) and a 'normal' child (N). The measurements (of height) obtained by the investigator could be as represented in Figure A1, where $E_1$ is the height of the early maturer in the first group, the 10 year olds, $N_3$ the height of the 'normal' child in the third group, the 14 year olds, etc.

Fig. A1    *Growth of height (cross-sectional study)*

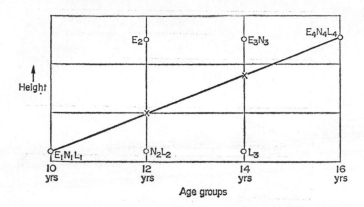

But the investigator is interested in average heights at each age, so he first calculates those average heights, shown by the Xs on Fig. A1, then he connects the average height of each age group and obtains the thick line of development shown. (Remember that since different children are measured at each age group, the experiment is over in an hour or so.)

Now consider another study, tackling the same problem, but using a longitudinal approach. This investigator chose three children aged 10 (who also happen to be one early maturer (e), one late maturer (l) and one normal child (n), and then measures *the same three children* once every two years. (Remember that this experiment lasts *six years*.) The information could be represented as in Figure A2.

Note that in this study, since he has used the same children throughout, the investigator can chart the development of each individual. He can also follow the line that the cross-sectional study *must* follow and chart the development of the *group* at each age level. This is the thick black line in Figure A2. But the important point to note is that during periods of growth the growth spurts of *individuals* are always much steeper than that of the group, and to reveal these individual rates, a longi-

Fig. A2    *Growth of height (longitudinal study)*

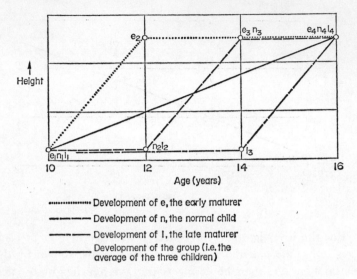

tudinal approach *must* be used. Hence the significance of the opportunity afforded by the main project to carry out an enquiry into the development of educational skills in a longitudinal context.

# Appendix B

*Emotional characteristics of the longitudinal sub-sample*

During the first and last terms of infant schooling class teachers were asked to complete questions about the child's adjustment to school. Some of the information for the case studies was drawn from two administrations of the Rutter Behaviour Questionnaire (Rutter 1967) which asked the teacher to rate each child on a series of behaviour problems, for example, 'Very restless; Often running about or jumping up and down; Hardly ever still.' The ratings were on a three point scale 'Doesn't apply', 'Applies somewhat', 'Certainly applies'. Although the ratings are dependent upon the subjective opinions of each teacher and rely upon her rating each child in relationship to all other children of the same age of which she has had experience, the scale as a whole has a high reliability when assessments are made by different people.

If the two ratings 'applies somewhat' and 'certainly applies' are taken together, children from schools in disadvantaged areas received 128(94)* mentions of behaviour problems compared with 37(61) in children from schools in advantaged areas. Of these, behaviour rated as 'certainly applies' occurred 44(16) times in children from schools in disadvantaged areas and 5(5)

* Numbers in brackets refer to the assessments made in the last term of infant schooling.

times in children from schools in advantaged areas. At the time of the first assessment 38 of all problems occurred in 5 of 7 children whose father had died or left home and 4 of these 7 were said to have poor concentration or a short attention span. However, by the time of the second assessment, only 2 of the 7 children were said to have any behaviour problems.

It would perhaps be expected that the total number of behaviour problems would diminish between the first and second assessments, as children are likely to have some difficulty in adjusting to the school situation at first, although the problems this creates are not usually long lasting. But it is noticeable that whereas the number of problems and the intensity of these problems for children in disadvantaged schools decreased, the problems for children in advantaged schools increased. This pattern becomes more interesting when one looks at the changes in specific areas of behaviour.

Within the total Rutter Scale are two sub-scales which are related to neurotic and anti-social behaviour. The distribution of these aspects of behaviour can be seen in Tables B1 and B2.

Other aspects of behaviour on which children from schools in disadvantaged areas scored highly were restlessness (11), thumb sucking (10) and disobedience (10). As would be expected, the incidence of neurotic and anti-social behaviour decreased overall, but whereas children from schools in disadvantaged areas were rated as less neurotic and considerably less anti-social by the time they were in their last term at the infant school, children from schools in advantaged areas were slightly more neurotic and certainly more anti-social. However, care should be taken in interpreting these results; when we look at children attending schools in advantaged, residential areas, it may well be that any anti-social behaviour is more noticeable and less acceptable than the same behaviour might be in schools where the expectations of behaviour are different.

The problems most mentioned by teachers at the time of the first assessment were disobedience (12), tears on arrival at

Table B1     *Distribution of behaviour problems by*
*school type—neurotic behaviour*

| Neurotic behaviour | Advantaged schools | Dis- advantaged schools | Total |
|---|---|---|---|
| 1 Often worried, worries about many things | 5 (7) | 8 (10) | 13 (17) |
| 2 Often appears miserable, unhappy, tearful or distressed | 2 (2) | 10 (8) | 12 (10) |
| 3 Tends to be fearful or afraid of new things or situations | 2 (4) | 9 (11) | 11 (15) |
| 4 Has had tears on arrival at school or has refused to come into the building | 3 (1) | 13 (0) | 16 (1) |
| Total | 12 (14) | 40 (29) | 52 (43) |

Note: Figures in brackets refer to assessments made in the
last term of infant schooling.

school (11), worrying (10), restlessness (9), poor concentration
(9), fearfulness (8), miserableness (8). At the time of the
second assessment the problems most mentioned were worrying (17), fearfulness (15), poor concentration (13), disobedience
(12), solitariness (12), miserableness (10). It is often said that
teachers are more aware of disruptive, anti-social behaviour
than they are of the problems of the shy, nervous child. However the above evidence does not confirm this view. It is interesting to compare these results with those of Chazan and
Jackson (1971) who examined the behaviour problems of 726

children aged 5.0–5.7. They found that significantly more of the deprived area group showed problems than did the middle-class sample, and there was a tendency for the deprived area children to show more restlessness and unsociability (lying, stealing, destructiveness etc.). Head teachers in these deprived area schools were particularly concerned about restlessness and aggressiveness.

Table B2    *Distribution of behaviour problems by school type—anti-social behaviour*

| Anti-social behaviour | Advantaged schools | Dis-advantaged schools | Total |
|---|---|---|---|
| 1 Often destroys own or others' belongings | 1 (1) | 2 (0) | 3 (1) |
| 2 Frequently fights with other children | 1 (5) | 8 (2) | 9 (7) |
| 3 Is often disobedient | 4 (7) | 10 (5) | 14 (12) |
| 4 Often tells lies | 2 (0) | 2 (0) | 4 (0) |
| 5 Has stolen things on one or more occasions | 0 (3) | 2 (0) | 2 (3) |
| 6 Bullies other children | 1 (4) | 3 (2) | 4 (6) |
| Total | 9 (20) | 27 (9) | 36 (29) |

Note: Figures in brackets refer to assessments made in the last term of infant schooling.

Although it is not possible to make direct comparisons with the results of Chazan and Jackson, because the same measures of behaviour problems were not used, the composition of both samples was very similar, although the longitudinal sub-sample was on a much smaller scale. The results of Chazan and Jackson are most comparable to the results obtained from the first administration of the Rutter Behaviour Questionnaire, when children in both samples were approximately the same age. At this time our findings are similar in that children from disadvantaged schools showed far more behaviour problems than children from advantaged schools (67 mentions as compared with 21) and were said to be more anti-social (27 mentions compared with 9). It is however interesting to note that at the time of the second administration of the scale the incidence of neurotic and anti-social behaviour problems in both types of school were roughly the same and children in advantaged schools were said to be more anti-social.

# Appendix C

*Difficulty levels of some phonic skills*

Teachers of reading may be interested in the relative difficulty which children find with the phonic elements tested. The sequence suggested by the standardization data of the test is displayed in Figure C.1.

Fig. C1   *Difficulty levels of phonic elements*

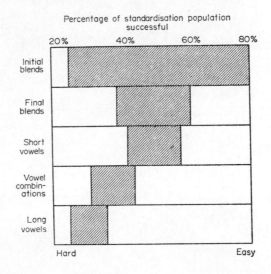

Note that the difficulty order revealed by the test is not the same as the teaching order suggested by a number of phonic schemes. Thus long vowels, which are often taught early, are among the last to be mastered.

It was not possible to determine the sequence in which the individual children of our sub-sample acquired these phonic skills. Undoubtedly there are differences between children which will need a different type of enquiry to explore.

Note also that this diagram is not intended to be a hard and fast reference to the difficulty level of the various phonic elements it displays. It merely records the observed difficulty order demonstrated in the 378 infant school children of the standardization population of the test used.

# References

Bloom, B. S. (1964), *Stability and Change in Human Characteristics*. New York: Wiley.

Chazan, M., and Jackson, S. (1971), 'Behaviour Problems in the Infant School'. *J. Child Psychol. Psychiat.*, **12**, 191–210.

Douglas, J. W. B. (1964), *The Home and the School*. London: MacGibbon and Kee.

Evans, R., 'Technical Manual to the Swansea Evaluation Profiles'. To be published by the Schools Council.

Evans, R., Davies, P., Ferguson, N., and Williams, P., 'Swansea Evaluation Profiles'. To be published by the Schools Council.

Otto, W., *et al.* (1972), 'Summary and Review of Investigations Relating to Reading. July 1st 1970–June 30th, 1971'. *J. Educational Research*, **65**, 6, Feb. 1972, 242–72.

Pringle, M. L., Kellmer, Butler, N. T., and Davie, R. (1966), *11,000 Seven Year-Olds: First Report of the National Child Development Study (1958 Cohort)*. London: Longman.

Raven, J. C. (1965), *Guide to using the Coloured Progressive Matrices*, Sets A, Ab, B. (Revised order 1956). London: H. K. Lewis.

Registrar General (1966), *Classification of Occupations*. London: H.M.S.O.

Rutter, M. (1967), 'A Children's Behaviour Questionnaire for Completion by Teachers: Preliminary Findings'. *J. Child Psychol. Psychiat.* **8**, 1–11.

Schonell, F. J., and Schonell, F. E. (1960), *Diagnostic and Attainment Testing*. Edinburgh: Oliver and Boyd.

Southgate, V. (1959), *Southgate Group Reading Tests: Test 1. Word Selection*. London: U.L.P.

Tanner (1961), *Education and Physical Growth: implications of the study of children's growth for educational theory and practice*. London University Press.

Williams, P. (1961), 'The Growth of Reading Vocabulary and some of its implications'. *Brit. J. Educ. Psychol.*, **31**, 1961, 104–5.

Williams, P. (1970), *The Swansea Test of Phonic Skills*. Oxford: Blackwell.